Survival Family Basics

Zombie Apocalypse

The Prepper's Guide to Pandemic Outbreak, Quarantine, and Zombie Fallout

I0427848

Macenzie Guiver

© 2014

Printed in the United States of America

Just to say Thank You for Purchasing this Book I want to give you a gift 100% absolutely FREE

A Copy of My Upcoming Special Report "The Prepper's Supplies Guide for When Disaster Strikes"

Go to www.SurvivalFamilyBasics.com to Sign Up to Receive Your FREE Gift

Table of Contents

Introduction

I want to thank you and congratulate you for downloading, *"Zombie Apocalypse: The Prepper's Guide to Pandemic Outbreak, Quarantine, and Zombie Fallout."*

Zombies are everywhere and to most people they are something out of scary stories like vampires or werewolves, no more real than Santa Claus or the Easter Bunny, but are we dismissing these blood-thirsty monsters at our peril? According to several scientists who have taken on the task of proving or disproving the possibility of zombies, while it is possible that some previously unknown disease could cause symptoms similar to those associated with pop-culture zombies, it is also unlikely.

But the actual disaster behind a zombie apocalypse, a global pandemic, is not only possible, it is likely and it is likely to happen during our lifetime.

This is why I put this guide together. Whether you buy into the idea that zombies could be real or not, there is no denying that a global pandemic poses a real risk to the safety and security of our families. And the only way to ensure your family survives the next pandemic is to start planning and preparing now.

The guide begins by explaining why you need to plan for a pandemic and then explains how a global pandemic starts and how it spreads. It covers some of the important lessons about pandemics that we can learn from history and how we can use those lessons to protect our families when the time comes. It explains how a global pandemic will affect life as we know it from the first few days until it eventually burns out. The guide wraps up by walking through the basics of creating a pandemic preparedness plan.

I hope this book will inspire you to use the zombie apocalypse as an interesting backdrop to start your pandemic preparedness plan.

Thanks again for downloading this book. I hope you enjoy it!

Macenzie Guiver

Why You Need to Be Worried about Zombies

When it comes to preppers believing in the possibility of zombies and the threat of a zombie apocalypse, I have found people are generally in one of two separate and very distinct groups. You either believe it is possible and therefore are serious about preparing for the day the dead roam the Earth or you think people who think that are silly and that they should go back to planning for real threats like an economic meltdown. But I think every prepper should take the threat of a zombie apocalypse as seriously as they do any other potential TEOTWAWKI (The End of the World as We Know It) scenario. Why? Because the most likely source of a zombie apocalypse would be a pandemic illness and regardless of whether or not that illness actually creates a horde of undead, someday it will come and if you aren't ready, you are the one who will look silly.

Now, before you put down this guide and stop reading, give me a chance to convince you that the zombie threat is real. Most preppers agree that the threat of a global pandemic is real and likely in their lifetime. Most epidemiologists, researchers, and experts in pandemic disease also agree that this is a real threat and that it will happen again. It is only a matter of time.

So, what does that have to do with zombies? Well, let's set aside the idea that a zombie is someone who has died and come back to life for a minute and regard zombieism simply as a set of symptoms. When you look at it this way, it becomes clear why the threat of zombies and the threat of pandemic are actually one and the same. Both involve a fast moving, highly infectious agent that is previously unknown to the medical community and that causes an untreatable, incurable illness. Both lead to a relatively quick breakdown of key pieces of our society's infrastructure. And both will be difficult to survive if you haven't taken the time and effort ahead of time to create a plan, stockpile the right supplies, obtain the right skills, and mentally prepare your family to deal with the immediate and long-term aftermath of this kind of catastrophic event.

With me so far? Good. Now, some of you might be thinking "Okay, so I think a pandemic is possible but with zombies you aren't just dealing with an illness that is trying to kill you, you are also dealing with all these undead creatures who are also trying to kill you. Doesn't that mean you need different kinds of preps for a zombie event than for an influenza pandemic?" The answer is simple. Regardless of the source of the pandemic, there will be other threats beyond the illness or disease itself. Does it really matter if the other things trying to kill you are coming after you because they want to eat your brains or because they want to eat your food stockpile? The threats are really the same, one of them is just a little easier to stomach and therefore easier to talk about and plan around.

In case you are wondering, the easier one has to be the zombies since having to fend off crazed monsters who are mindlessly pursuing meat because they have a disease is much easier to think about than having to fend off your neighbor who is threatening to shoot your child if you don't give up your water supply.

How Pandemics Happen

Whether you are genuinely worried about zombies or not, you need to be worried about the looming threat of a global pandemic. I am a student of history and I think there are many lessons we, as modern-day prepping families, can learn from the pandemics of the past that will help us keep our families safe no matter what we face in the future.

In order to effectively plan for a pandemic, even one featuring meat-seeking, half crazed creatures that look like your former neighbors, you need to have a basic understanding of what causes a pandemic, where they come from, and how they happen. The first we need to establish is that when we talk about prepping for a global pandemic what we really mean is prepping for the aftermath of one that has been deadly enough to impact daily life. Most of us have already lived through at least two pandemics, even if we don't realize it.

First, you survived the most recent pandemic which occurred in 2009 and was caused by Swine Flu. Second, you have thus far survived the ongoing AIDs pandemic which has been going on since the mid 1980's. These two outbreaks bring up a very important point – not all pandemics are created equal. Not everyone has the potential to wipe out half the world's population or cause a breakdown in essential services. In fact, there have actually been 4 separate global pandemics since the last great one in the early days of the last century that have come and gone without causing a disruption in society.

This simply means that you need to be able to differentiate between a pandemic and a pandemic that will bring about TEOTWAWKI, at least for a period of time. So, how can you tell the difference? Let's look at what it would take from outbreak to aftermath for a zombie-like pandemic to develop.

The Disease

To start with, we would need a disease, but not just any disease will do. There are a few important characteristics that our zombie disease will have to have in order for it to cause a society disrupting global pandemic.

First, it has to be something new, some disease we have never seen before. There are two reasons for this. The obvious reason is that we haven't ever experienced a zombie-like disease which means.... it has to be new. But more importantly, from a pandemic perspective, it has to be new so that the medical community is not equipped to diagnose, treat, cure, or vaccinate against it. The spread of a pandemic depends in part on its ability to spread faster than our ability to stop it from spreading. If it is a disease we have seen before, scientists have studied it, any possible treatments or vaccines have been developed, and we know enough about it to try and stop it from spreading.

Next, it needs to be highly contagious. Again, pandemics happen when a disease spreads faster than we can respond to its spread. In order to outpace things like quarantine protocols and border closures, our disease has to be easily transmissible from one person to another. This generally means that it would be airborne or waterborne. However, most stories about zombies indicate that zombieism is spread through bites, kind of like rabies. This implies that our disease would have to be transmissible through contact with blood or other bodily fluids. While this does make it more difficult to create a pandemic, it isn't impossible, especially if the sole objective of those who become infected becomes infecting others. However, since this is a new disease that no one has seen before, our disease is going to be transmissible through casual contact which means it is the worst thing any infectious disease can be – airborne.

The next thing our disease needs is a good starting point. The first outbreak has to happen in a place where there are a lot of people. Otherwise, there is a greater chance that society will be able to stop the spread by quarantining the area where the outbreak occurs. This is one of the reasons that some of the nastiest diseases we know like Ebola have never been considered high risk for pandemic. They generally occur in very remote areas which are easy to quarantine and contain. Ideally, our disease would have an outbreak in an urban center with a significant amount of international travel so that the likelihood of someone who is infected traveling outside the outbreak area before quarantine protocols are established is relatively high.

Our disease also needs an incubation period during which the infected person is contagious but not symptomatic. Essentially, our disease needs to be able to spread before anyone, even the person who is infected, even realizes it exists. Again, this is all about spreading far enough and fast enough to outpace humanities efforts at containment.

It will also need to be deadly, but it cannot kill people off too quickly unless the incubation period is pretty long and people are contagious from the minute they become exposed. It needs to be deadly because in order to experience the kinds of societal disruption that would require preparedness, enough people need to be removed from society to cause a breakdown in essential services. But, it can't kill people too quickly or it will burn out before it can achieve the distribution needed to cause a catastrophic global event. This is the other primary reason that Ebola has never been a real candidate for a potential pandemic. It simply kills too many people too quickly to spread very far. However, if the incubation period was long enough for an infected person to infect enough other people before they became symptomatic, the speed at which our disease killed would be less relevant.

So, to sum up, our zombie-like global pandemic disease has to be new and very contagious with an initial outbreak in an urban area and a long, asymptomatic incubation period. It needs to have a high fatality rate but unless the incubation period allows for significant spread of the disease prior to the onset of symptoms, it can't kill too quickly or it will burn out before TEOTWAWKI.

Oh, and one more thing. It has to be difficult to treat and a vaccine must be difficult to develop for it. This means our disease is probably going to be a virus which can't be treated with antibiotics and which constantly mutates making vaccine development nearly impossible.

The Outbreak

Now that we have a disease, we need an outbreak. As previously stated, it would be best if the outbreak occurred in an urban area where there are a lot of people. If that urban area is also a global business hub like London, New York, or Hong Kong, that would be even better because that means there will be a lot of people moving in and out of the area in the initial days of the outbreak.

If we were picking the ideal country where our zombie-like disease would emerge and break out, China would have to top the list. The reason China would be the best place for a new zombie virus to emerge is that it checks all "easily spread global pandemic" boxes. It has a large population and several urban centers that have large amounts of global travelers moving in and out of them every day. It also has a secretive government and a censored press which would be incredibly beneficial in keeping the emergence of a new, frightening disease under wraps.

Just look at what happened with SARS (Severe Acute Respiratory Syndrome), a novel coronavirus that caused headlines and almost 800 deaths in early 2003. The first case of SARS is believed to have been a Chinese farmer who died in November 2002. As other people fell ill in the same province, the Chinese government tried, ineffectively, to deal with the spread of the new disease. Rumors about a new kind of flu circulating in the country prompted the World Health Organization and other global health agencies to prod China for more information in December 2002 and January 2003. But the Chinese government refused to cooperate or allow international involvement until an American died of the disease after visiting China in February of 2003. It would take two more months to identify the SARS virus genome and prove it was the cause of the outbreak. It would take an additional month for researchers to determine the source of the disease in order to impose protocols to help stop new infections and halt the diseases spread.

Given that, even though the Chinese government appears to be more willing to work with the global health community, imagine what would happen if there was an outbreak of a new disease that caused people to attack and try to eat each other.

The Spread

Alright, our new zombie-like disease has started to infect people in China. To demonstrate how a pandemic virus can spread, let's make up some numbers and do a little math.

First, our disease needs an incubation period. Let's use 14 days which is average for most infectious diseases.

Next, we need to decide how long our disease is latent. This means how long it takes for a person who has been infected to become contagious. To make the math easy, we are going to assume people are contagious from the minute they become infected.

We also need something called the R_0 or r-nought. This is the number of people that each infected person is likely to infect. This number varies wildly across different infectious diseases and is determined with a large amount of data that only becomes available after an outbreak begins. For our purposes, we are going to use an R_0 of 5-7 which is similar to the R_0 of many other infectious diseases. This means that for every person who becomes infected, 5-7 other people will become infected.

To track the spread of the disease, we need a patient zero or the first person to contract the disease. Our disease is going to start with a farmer who lives in a rural area. The closest urban center to our patient zero is Shanghai which happens to be one of the major hubs for international travel in Asia. Our farmer contracts the disease and gives it to his wife two days before his adult children come home for a visit. He has four children that are all married and that each have 1 child and they stay for 2 days. Each of the 12 family members visiting contract the disease and take it back to their own cities and towns when they leave.

- Day 1-4: Patient 0 infects 7 people = 8 total infections
- Day 2-4: Patient 0 Wife infects 6 people = 14 total infections

Upon returning to their homes, each of the family members who were infected in turn infects another 6 people each and those 6 people infect another 6 people.

- Day 4-8: Patient 0 family members infect 72 people = 86 total infections
- Day 8-12: 72 x 6 new infections = 432 + previously infected = 518 total infections

Each of the 432 newly infected people spread the disease to 6 more people each.

- Day 12-16: 432 x 6 new infections =2,592 + previously infected = 3,110 total infections

On Days 14 and 15, the farmer and his wife start showing symptoms and after attacking their family doctor, they are restrained and taken to the hospital in Shanghai. At first, the doctors treating them think it is some variant of rabies because of the symptoms and the tendency to bite people. But when they administer the rabies vaccine, it has no effect. While in the hospital, the farmer and his wife each infect 5 health care workers by biting them and those 10 continue to spread the disease to other patients in the hospital.

At this point, you may be wondering why the farmer and his wife are infecting more people than the 5-7 determined by the R_0. This is to highlight that not everyone will infect the same amount of people. In the early days, people are likely to infect a higher number because the doctors don't know what it is or what precautions to take.

About a week after the farmer enters the hospital, he dies. At this point, around Day 21, assuming the disease continues to spread at the same, somewhat unrealistic rate of 6 new infections per infected every 4 days there will be around 100,000 people infected. However, since only about 100-200 of the infected have become symptomatic, no alerts have been given and no one is investigating the emergence of the new disease.

Within the next week, days 21-28, patients begin arriving at hospitals in other parts of the world. Reports of a new mysterious disease make headlines around the world and the global health community starts investigating. Unfortunately, despite the fact that we are only a little more than three weeks into the pandemic, it is too late to try and stop the spread. By the end of that first month, more than a million people all over the world will be infected.

The Aftermath

Now, remember what happened with SARS. Once the global health community learned about the new disease, it took two months to establish which virus was causing the illness and it took a third month to determine the source of the outbreak. Even if the rate of infection slowed once the global alert went out and only 5 new infections occurred for each infected every 7 days, there would still be more than 18 million people infected within 6 weeks of the initial infection and 4 weeks of the first symptomatic case showing up at a hospital.

And despite continued decreases in the rate and speed of infection over the following 10 week period (which is how long it took to identify the source of the SARS outbreak) the number of infected would skyrocket to more than 750 million.

To put that in perspective, the great influenza pandemic of 1918 infected 500 million people over a period of 2 years. Our disease has infected 1.5 times that many in only 4 months and that is assuming that infection rates are going down beginning at the 6 week mark. But there is a sound argument to be made that with a disease like this one, where people are driven to bite other people, there would come a point at which there were too many symptomatic people to exert enough control over the infected to keep them from infecting others. Basically, at some point, there won't be enough hospital beds with restraints, jail cells, etc. to contain the infected and the infection rate might soar as those infected who cannot be contained roam around attacking those who aren't infected.

If we assume this to be true, the breaking point is likely to happen between the 6th and 8th week of the pandemic when the total number of infected worldwide soars to 75 million and the number that are symptomatic passes the 4 million mark. And, as they say, it is all downhill from there. Even with border closures, the suspension of air travel, and the closing of ports, we won't have any way to stop or control this disease; our only option will be to wait for it to burn itself out.

To understand what this will mean for us and our families, we need only take a look back at what history has to teach us.

What History has to Teach Us

One of the greatest unknowns when it comes to planning or prepping for the next catastrophic pandemic is how different a modern pandemic will be as compared to global pandemics in the past.

On one hand, the last catastrophic global pandemic was at the very beginning of the advances in medical science that led to modern medicine. In 1918, when the Spanish Flu killed as many as 100 million people, we didn't have penicillin and our understanding of germ theory and the affect of basic sanitation on infection control were only in their infancy. We didn't have an outbreak alert system or a good understanding of disease prevention. In many cases, medical professionals did things they thought would help their patients that we would consider to be the exact opposite of what should be done.

For this reason, there is every reason to assume that a global pandemic, even one that featured a novel disease, would be easier to control than it would have been for people in the past. We have experts in infectious disease, entire government and global agencies dedicated to studying, understanding, and stopping the spread of infectious disease, and, unlike our ancestors, we know without question that this kind of pandemic is going to happen again.

However, more than just our understanding of medicine has changed in the past 100 years. In 1918, people did not travel by airplane and even though the initial stages of urban migration had begun, more people still lived in rural areas than in urban centers. Most people didn't have a car which means things like commuting to another city or town everyday wasn't something people did. Our lives were much smaller and most of us rarely left the area where we were born and raised.

There were also a lot fewer of us in 1918 than there are today. The global population in 1918 was about 1.8 billion people. Today, there are about 7.2 billion people on the planet. This means we are living closer together and that there are more of us available to carry a pathogen to the far corners of the planet. We are more mobile and more interconnected than any past society and when it comes to the next pandemic, some of the greatest advances in the last 100 years may mean the aftermath of a pandemic, even one of the same relative size as the 1918 event, could have much more significant consequences.

The Spanish Flu

The last great pandemic was caused by the H1N1 influenza virus and was called the Spanish Flu. The first documented case of what would become known as the Spanish Flu was observed in a rural part of Kansas in January of 1918. Although historians believe that the virus may actually have originated in China. Evidence indicates that it may actually have been introduced to American troops on the European front in late 1917 by Chinese laborers. These soldiers then returned to the U.S., bringing the virus with them, where it mutated into the more deadly strain that was responsible for the pandemic the following year.

On March 11, 1918, the disease suddenly gained a foothold at a Kansas military base and more than 100 men reported sick within the first 6 hours of the day. Within days, there were more than 500 men with the illness on that single base but by that time, the illness had already begun appearing in other places.

Over the course of that spring, the illness would make its way around the country and cross the Atlantic Ocean with the soldiers heading to Europe to fight in World War I. Some believe that one of the reasons this pandemic was so deadly in comparison to other pandemics was the dire living conditions experienced by soldiers fighting on the front lines. But the Spanish Flu didn't only kill soldiers who were tired, underfed, and living in horrible conditions. It killed people back home as well.

In fact, one of the most frightening things about the Spanish Flu is that it killed the people that are usually the least likely to die from this kind of disease, the young healthy people between 20 and 50. Unlike other illnesses then and now which are generally more dangerous to the very old and the very young, the Spanish Flu killed those in the prime of life who were in good health. And when it killed those people, it killed them quickly, often in less than 24 hours.

The pandemic came in two waves, one in the spring and one in the fall. The fall wave was much more virulent as the virus had mutated to become more deadly. Overall, the Spanish Flu infected 500 million people, one third of the world's population. It killed between 50 and 100 million people, as much as 20% of those it infected.

And many experts believe that the constant movement of troops and the close quarters caused by the war contributed to the extremely high infection rate.

So, what does that mean for us and our zombie disease?

Well, the troop movements of World War I are nothing compared to the sheer mobility of modern society. Almost twice as many people will fly on a plane this year as existed on the planet during that pandemic. To me, this means that the increase in infection rate attributed to the movement of troops was just a precursor to the kind of rates we would see today with a novel disease that was as infectious as the virus that caused the Spanish Flu.

Additionally, some experts believe that the Spanish Flu killed 25 million people in its first 25 weeks without airplanes transporting people to distant parts of the world in a matter of hours and with a quarter of our current population. Without accounting for any other factors, that would equate to the death of almost 100 million people between the beginning of March and the end of August. And that wasn't even the deadliest part of the pandemic.

If you were struggling to believe that 750 million people could be infected with our new zombie virus in the first 4 months, think about this. If our disease mirrored the 1918 pandemic and we simply adjust the numbers to account for the differences in population, 2.3 billion people would be infected by the virus before the pandemic ended and 460 million people would die.

But what about the advances in modern medicine we have made since 1918? Won't our increased understanding of infectious diseases and how to control them make a difference?

Yes, maybe, at least in the beginning. But all the modern medicine in the world won't matter once the number of people who need medical care begins to outpace our capacity to provide it. This is especially true when you consider that people who provide medical care like doctors and nurses are likely to be some of the first to become infected as they will be interacting with the earliest cases without a full understanding of what they are dealing with.

One of the things 1918 taught us is that hospitals and medical facilities will quickly be overtaxed and the standard of care will quickly degrade as the number of infected increases. This means that while we will have the benefit of our advanced understanding of infection control measures on our side, much of what we would look to from modern medicine to save lives, like respirators and even antibiotics to treat secondary infections will be largely unavailable.

History also teaches us that it doesn't take a major disaster to cause catastrophic consequences. The earthquake in Haiti, Hurricane Katrina, the Syrian Civil War, all of these events had a ripple effect beyond the actual damage caused by the disaster or conflict. And in truth, while prepping to survive the next pandemic, whether it comes with zombies or not, has to be your first preparedness objective when it comes to pandemic planning, that is, unfortunately, only the beginning.

What Happens When a Pandemic Strikes

We can also learn lessons about the potential aftermath of a pandemic from the pages of history. Let's dive into the kinds of societal impacts we should expect to experience in the days, weeks, and months following the next pandemic.

The First Few Weeks

One of the first things that will happen as the world realizes there is a new deadly disease racing around the globe is that international travel will be disrupted. Agencies like the World Health Organization will begin issuing recommendations restricting travel to certain locations. But it won't be long before countries begin voluntarily closing their international airports to incoming flights to keep the new disease out.

Another thing that will happen in the first few weeks is border closures. In an effort to slow the spread of the disease and to help protect their own populations, countries, provinces, states, and even cities and towns will close their borders. People will not be able to enter or leave. This was effective with the SARS outbreak in 2003 but only because the virus spread slowly in the beginning. A faster moving disease will easily outpace our ability to contain it, especially if it has a long incubation period that allows people to spread the disease before they are symptomatic, like our zombie disease.

Medical facilities here in the U.S. will be able to keep up with the flow of patients for the first few weeks but will become inundated as the number of new patients grows day after day. Other facilities like stadiums, schools, warehouses, and private facilities will be commandeered for use as makeshift hospitals. Medical supplies, specifically those needed to prevent the spread of infectious disease like gowns, gloves, and masks will begin to run out. Desperation will quickly set in as people realize they cannot get any help for their loved ones who are sick. Loss of access to medical care will spur the first bouts of civil unrest as grief-stricken, desperate people seek to get the things they need for their families at any cost.

Store shelves will quickly be emptied of staples and medical supplies but they will be able to be replenished to some degree for at least the first few weeks. However, border closures and absenteeism across the supply chain will rapidly erode the capacity to move goods around the country. It won't be long before average citizens are forced to rely on whatever government assistance can be provided simply to satisfy basic needs.

The Months Ahead

Once it becomes clear that closing borders and ending air travel isn't working, strict quarantine procedures will be put in place. Sick individuals may be forcibly removed from their homes, taken from their families and relocated to crowded quarantine facilities to try and stem the tide of infection. This will only increase the incidence of civil unrest as armed individuals use force to stop their family members from being taken or in an attempt to free them from the quarantine facility.

As the number of infected, sick, and dead grows, schools will close, businesses will close, and commerce as we know it will slow to a crawl. More and more people begin to stay home because they are ill, to care for the ill, or to try and keep from becoming ill. Absenteeism will cause issues with all basic services including mail delivery, trash pickup, delivery services, movement of freight, and even utilities. There simply won't be enough people well enough to work or willing to leave their homes and families to keep everything going.

The flow of goods across the country and around the world will all but stop. A combination of quarantine protocols, border closures, and rampant absenteeism will make it impossible to load trucks, transport goods, unload trucks, or stock shelves. Delivery of everything from food to fuel will become erratic at best. People will not be able to get gas for their cars, fuel oil for their homes, or food for their families. Looting and rioting will become frequent occurrences as people's desperation for supplies overtakes their fear of infection.

Wide-spread outages of essential services like electricity, water, sewer, and telephone will result from widespread absenteeism in these areas. Without enough people to monitor the utilities, repair lines, and service customers, access to power, running water, and even working toilets will be erratic.

Ambulances and coroner's vans will struggle to transport the dead as the number of bodies needing burial increases day after day. Funeral homes and cemeteries will be inundated, shutting down to avoid rioting or because they don't have enough healthy employees to continue operations. We won't have enough body bags to hold the dead. Families will have to bury their family member themselves or leave them by the side of the road in the hopes that they will be picked up and buried in a mass grave somewhere.

The National Guard is deployed in many states to help enforce quarantine and curfews, distribute supplies, and prevent looting and rioting. The loss of services and lack of access to supplies will drive many people into shelters and refugee camps operated by local, state, and federal agencies.

Unfortunately, this could jumpstart a second wave of the pandemic as large groups of people are brought together in close quarters with limited access to running water and basic sanitation.

The accumulation of trash, the large numbers of unburied bodies, and the loss of some essential services creates a whole new health crisis as common disaster diseases like cholera, hepatitis A, E. coli, and typhoid begin to spread through quarantine camps, shelters, and hospitals.

For many people, this is at least a temporary TEOTWAWKI. Without stores to shop in, running water, basic sanitation, or access to routine or emergency medical care, people are mostly left to fend for themselves. Some will remain in their homes and manage as best they can, others will take to the streets using violence to get the things they need, others will risk going to the camps in exchange for basic supplies and some sense of security.

The human and economic toll of the pandemic will be catastrophic. But even the worst pandemic disease will eventually burn itself out. Although the 1918 pandemic technically lasted for about a year, the infection and death rates peaked in the fall during the second deadlier wave. Death rates dropped sharply in November of that year and for the first time, things started to get better. It took time to rebuild the economy, restore all essential services, and get people back to living more normal lives, but it did happen. This is the good news. The bad news is that that recovery will take time. And it is dependent on the pandemic burning out because it mutates to a less virulent form or because there aren't enough susceptible people left to sustain the spread of infection.

Both of those are fine assumptions to make if the pandemic we are dealing with is caused by a strain of influenza or even a novel coronavirus like the one that caused SARS in 2003 or the more recently discovered MERS. But how would things be different if the disease behind the pandemic was something like our zombie disease?

Why Zombies Would Be Worse

Most of the previous section speaks to the aftermath of a "standard" pandemic caused by influenza or a similar virus if there can ever be such a thing. But if the disease causing the pandemic is our zombie disease, would that change the impacts and the outlook? Unfortunately, based on the set of symptoms we are working with, we have to say yes. A zombie pandemic would be worse and here is why.

1. It would take precious time for governments and global agencies to come to terms with the fact that this disease doesn't debilitate those who are infected the same way that something like the flu would. When someone is sick with the flu, they are exhausted and unlikely to be mobile which actually helps keep the disease from spreading. But our zombie disease may actually increase the activity level of the infected once they become symptomatic as they are driven to attack others.

2. The fact that once someone becomes symptomatic they are driven to attack others and to bite them could significantly increase the R_0 for our disease. A higher R_0 means a faster spread and higher infection rate. If the disease spreads faster and infects higher numbers, all the impacts above happen much more quickly.

3. Simply dealing with a large group of people who need medical care but who must also be restrained will put

additional stress on the hospitals, medical staff, police, and military units dispatched to deal with the pandemic.

4. Families caring for infected family members will also struggle to keep those people restrained and there will be high rates of accidental infection to anyone caring for someone who has the disease.

5. With a standard pandemic, those who have the disease are generally too sick to be very mobile, but if our zombie disease makes people sick without incapacitating them, it is entirely possible that hordes of infected will not be able to be contained and will roam around attacking people. This will make people afraid to leave their homes at all.

6. We will be faced with a moral dilemma when the number of uncontained infected threatens to overwhelm those who are not infected. Choices will have to be made around whether or not it is ethical to kill those who are infected in order to save those who are not. Remember, unlike the zombies in the movies, our "zombies" are not the dead come back to life. They are simply people suffering from a disease. This is a difficult ethical question to answer at any time but when governments are barely operational and everyone is stretched to the limit, it will be harder to put morality and ethics ahead of survival.

7. Although we can hope for a mutation that will end the pandemic, assuming our zombie disease is a virus, we may not be able to rely on it burning out on its own in order for the pandemic to end. One of the reasons other pandemics burn out is that people who are stricken get better and their new immunity helps protect others who have not been infected. The

smaller the pool of susceptible people, the harder it is for the disease to spread. This is how herd immunity provided by vaccines works today. But what if there is no cure for the zombie disease? If it is like rabies, which is actually the closest modern day disease in terms of symptoms and method of transmission to the classic view of zombie-ism, people won't recover from it. Becoming infected will be a death sentence until such time as a vaccine, like the one we have for rabies, is developed. That will take months at best but is more likely to take years. In the meantime, those who have been infected will continue to infect others.

What You Need to Do Now

With that dire picture in place, let's shift the focus to something a little more hopeful – what you can do to get your family ready for the next global pandemic.

Basic Pandemic Planning

Regardless of whether the next pandemic creates teeth-chomping zombies or gives people a deadly version of the flu, the first thing you need to do to keep your family safe is to develop your basic pandemic plan. This will help you ensure you have the resources, supplies, and skills you will need to withstand even a zombie pandemic.

Take Stock
The first step is to take stock of what you have. Odds are you are already prepping for other major disasters and understanding what you already have in place will streamline your pandemic planning process. Make sure you are taking an inventory of all your preps including food, water, medical supplies, and the skill sets of those in your family or survival group.

Decide When to Move
Next, you need to decide how you will respond in the first few days following the emergence of a novel disease with pandemic potential. For most people, the answer will be to watch and wait. As we saw with the 2009 Swine Flu pandemic, some diseases can race around the globe without devastating everything in their path. But if you have the flexibility to take action as soon as a new disease emerges (you work for yourself, home school your children, etc.), you may choose to implement part of your pandemic plan as soon as you know about a potential threat.

In truth, deciding when to act may be the most challenging part of creating and implementing your pandemic plan. On one hand, you don't want to jump the gun. You want to avoid calling out of work or yanking your kids out of school too soon. Most of the time, discovery of a novel disease will wind up being like the Swine Flu pandemic or like the more recent emergence of influenza strain H7N9 which is serious but isn't easily passed from person to person which limits its ability to spread. On the other hand, every day that you wait increases the chances that someone in your family will be exposed. If you look back at the example of our zombie disease, it is easy to see how quickly a new, highly transmissible disease can travel before we even know it exists. If the disease has a long, contagious incubation period, people in your city or town could be infected before patient 0 even becomes symptomatic.

Where Will You Stay
I say this because the only real option for pandemic survival is to shelter in place, completely cutting yourself and your family off from the outside world until the threat has passed. So, as part of deciding when to make this retreat, you will also want to decide where you will go. Depending on where you live, part of your pandemic plan may involve bugging out. If you live in a city or even a suburban area, this is likely the best option for your long term survival. Remember, fewer people not only means less chance of infection, it also means you are less likely to have to deal with looters, rioting, and even hordes of infected people looking for someone to attack.

For other people, this is the perfect example of a time that you would want to shelter in place. Whichever way you choose, you will want to create a step by step plan for what will need to happen to secure your family once the decision is made that it is time to retreat. Since I have already talked extensively about bugging out in *The Prepper's Bug-Out Guide to Surviving on the Move When Disaster Strikes,* I am not going to cover bugging out to a bug-out location here. However, whether you are staying in your home or bugging out, the processes below for creating your own quarantine and sheltering in place are the same once you are in the location you plan to remain in for the duration of the pandemic.

Sheltering in Place

Sheltering in place or SIP, if you are not familiar with it, basically means to hole up where you are and to remain in that location until the current threat has passed. We use sheltering in place for a variety of circumstances in prepping and it is completely appropriate when the threat is an active pandemic.

In order to shelter in place, you will need to have all the supplies required to survive for an extended period of time on hand before the threat begins. This is because your goal is to be able to stay in your location, and possibly inside your house, for as long as you have to in order to remain safe. So, if your long term prepping plans involve you accessing the woods around your bug out location or collecting water from a stream near your home, you may need to put some other solution in place for your pandemic plan. The degree to which this is required will really depend on where you plan to SIP. If you are going to a remote area where you have 50 acres of empty forest all around you, it may not be as important that you don't have to leave the house. But if you will be sheltering anywhere close to other people, you need to have a plan to remain inside as much as possible and a means to venture outside safely if that is something you have to do.

Pandemic Specific Supplies

Long term survival supplies like food, water, fuel, etc. are covered in several other guides so I am not going to go into them here beyond stating that you need to have them on hand. But there are some supplies you will need for your pandemic preparedness plan that you may not already have in your prepper stash because they are very specific to the dangers posed by a pandemic. Here are some of the supplies I consider to be critical for any family that is prepping for a pandemic.

Protective Gear
This includes coveralls, latex gloves, eye protection, and face masks. While it is always going to be preferable to remain inside as much as possible, you need to have the supplies needed to leave your house without risking infection on hand before the pandemic starts. These supplies will rapidly fly off the shelves in the first few days so don't wait to add them to your stockpile. This kind of gear will also make it possible for you to care for someone who is sick without risking exposure.

Quarantine Protocol
If there is any chance that someone in your family has been infected prior to you sheltering in place, you need to set-up your own quarantine area that allows you to keep those who could be infected separate from those who are not. Creating a quarantine area can also be beneficial if you plan on allowing anyone else into your shelter after you have locked things down. For example, if you have family members who will join you from out of state if things get really bad, you can set-up a quarantine area inside your home that provides them with protection and shelter without risking exposure to your family.

In order to effectively use an in-home quarantine area, you will need a place that can be accessed from the outside, that has some basic sanitation facilities like a sink and a toilet, and that can be completely closed off using heavy duty plastic from the rest of the house. Don't forget to block off any air vents that are shared between the quarantine space and your living space in case the disease is airborne. Stock your quarantine space with non-perishable food, water, clean clothes, alternative light sources, and bedding. Write out the protocol for your quarantine and print it out so that you can place a copy of it in the area for newcomers to review.

The most important things you will need to successfully operate an in-house quarantine area are people willing to following the quarantine protocols, an understanding of the diseases lifecycle and incubation period, and patience. Additionally, if the pandemic is caused by something like our zombie disease, you will need to add something to your quarantine protocol about keeping watch. The last thing you need is for someone who is infected to become symptomatic while everyone in the house is sleeping with only a thick sheet of plastic and some duct tape to protect you.

Decontamination Supplies
In addition to isolating your family and setting up a quarantine area, you will also need a way to decontaminate people and things that have been outside the "safe area" so that you can bring them inside. Fortunately, one of the most effective substances for decontamination is likely something you already have in your preps – household bleach. When it comes to killing almost any disease on the planet, bleach is the best tool for eradication. Make sure you have an area for decontamination that is also separate from your living space. This area should allow you to remove any protective gear, decontaminate that gear, and decontaminate any supplies you are bringing into the home before re-entering your living space.

Supplementing Essential Services
In addition to basic long term supplies like food, water, and medicine, and those supplies specific to dealing with disease, you will also need to have a plan for handling the loss of essential services. While it is not a foregone conclusion that you will lose power or running water or heat in the aftermath

of a pandemic, there is a good enough chance that these things will happen that you need to be ready to deal with them.

At a minimum, you need to be able to handle basic sanitation needs like hand washing, food preparation, and going to the bathroom without electricity or running water.

Practicing Your Plan
Once you have your plan in place and your supplies on hand, you should run a few pandemic drills. Practicing setting up a quarantine area or getting your gear on will help you ensure that you haven't forgotten anything important. It will also make it easier to do these things in the midst of a crisis when your family members are scared and time is of the essence.

Additionally, although I didn't cover it here, you will want to take the time to ensure you have a plan for defending your location. There will be looters, rioters, infected, and just people desperate to survive in the weeks and months following an outbreak and your family's survival may depend on your ability to keep them from coming in. If you need more information about creating a home defense strategy and plan, you can pick up my guide called **The Hunkering Down Guide to Protect and Defend Your Home When Disaster Strikes.**

Conclusion

Could a zombie apocalypse like the one portrayed in the popular TV series *"The Walking Dead"* or the movie *"World War Z"* actually happen? There is no way to know for sure until it does, but there is a chance, even if it is relatively small, that some highly contagious virus could mutate in such a way that it produces zombie-like symptoms. However, I can tell you with certainty that there will be another catastrophic global pandemic similar to the one experienced in 1918. And there is every reason to believe that pandemic will happen during our lifetime.

That is why I wrote this guide. Whether the threat comes from a zombie disease or some errant strain of influenza, the threat of pandemic is real and it is something that every family must be prepared to handle in order to survive. When the 1918 flu swept around the globe, entire families and neighborhoods were wiped out. You would have been hard pressed to find anyone in civilization that hadn't lost someone to the disease. The only way to ensure the safety and survival of your family is to take steps now so that you are prepared when the next pandemic begins its race around the world.

Taking the time now to think about when to pull away from society and how to handle infection control and in-house quarantine will make it easier to do these difficult things quickly and efficiently when the risk of doing them wrong or taking too long might mean a death sentence for someone you love.

From providing an understanding of how pandemics progress from patient 0 to global catastrophe to explaining how a global pandemic will affect the society around us, this guide provides prepping families with the perspective, information, and planning steps they need to be ready to survive the next pandemic, even if that means fighting off zombies in order to do so!

Happy Prepping!

Macenzie

Check out these other *Survival Family Basics* Titles...

http://www.amazon.com/dp/B00HG7Y4YS

http://www.amazon.com/dp/B00KQXPZVA

http://www.amazon.com/dp/B00KNAYA30

http://www.amazon.com/dp/B00J1VGJXG

http://www.amazon.com/dp/B00J1V939S

http://www.amazon.com/dp/B00JXU7OBG

http://www.amazon.com/dp/B00K00DMQEa

http://www.amazon.com/dp/B00HYQ55W6